Campbell's®

contents

sloppy giuseppe's

prep time: 15 minutes | **total time:** 45 minutes | **makes** 6 servings

- 2 packages (10 ounces **each**) Pepperidge Farm® Garlic Bread
- 2 tablespoons olive oil
- 1 medium onion, diced (about ½ cup)
- 2 cloves garlic, minced
- 1 pound ground beef
- 1½ cups Prego® Flavored with Meat Italian Sauce
- ¾ cup shredded Cheddar cheese

1. Heat the oven to 400°F. Remove the bread from the bags. Carefully separate the bread halves with a fork. Place the bread halves, cut-side up, onto 2 baking sheets.

2. Bake the bread for 10 minutes or until heated through. Cut each baked bread loaf into thirds.

3. While the oven is heating, start the filling mixture. Heat the oil in a 12-inch skillet over medium heat. Add the onion and cook until tender. Add the garlic and cook and stir for 30 seconds. Add the beef and cook until well browned, stirring often to separate meat. Pour off any fat.

4. Stir in the sauce. Reduce the heat to medium-low. Cover and cook for 10 minutes or until the beef is cooked through. Season to taste. Divide the beef mixture among the 6 bottom bread pieces. Top with the cheese and the remaining bread pieces.

shepherd's pie

prep time: 20 minutes | **total time:** 35 minutes | **makes** 4 servings

1 pound ground beef

1 medium onion, chopped (about ½ cup)

1 can Campbell's® Condensed Cream of Mushroom Soup **or** Campbell's® Condensed 98% Fat Free Cream of Mushroom Soup

1 tablespoon ketchup

⅛ teaspoon ground black pepper

1 cup frozen peas and carrots

2½ cups reduced fat (2%) milk

¼ cup (½ stick) butter

2 cups instant mashed potato flakes **or** buds

1. Heat the oven to 400°F.

2. Cook the beef and onion in a 10-inch skillet over medium-high heat until the beef is well browned, stirring often to separate meat. Pour off any fat.

3. Stir the soup, ketchup, black pepper and peas and carrots in the skillet. Spoon the beef mixture into a 9-inch pie plate.

4. Heat milk and butter in 2-quart saucepan over medium-high heat to a boil. Remove the saucepan from the heat. Stir in the potatoes. The potatoes will be stiff. Spoon the potatoes over the beef mixture.

5. Bake for 15 minutes or until the potatoes are lightly browned.

tip| Try this Mexican-seasoned version with sour cream—Cheddar potatoes on top! Increase the ketchup to 2 tablespoons and the black pepper to 1 teaspoon. Reduce the milk to 2 cups. Substitute frozen corn for the peas and carrots. Add 1 poblano pepper, seeded and diced, to the beef mixture in Step 2. Add 1 envelope (about 1 ounce) taco seasoning mix to the soup mixture in Step 3. Stir in ½ cup sour cream and ¾ cup shredded Cheddar cheese with the potato flakes in Step 4. Spoon the potatoes over the beef mixture. Sprinkle with an additional ¼ cup shredded Cheddar cheese. Bake for 20 minutes or until the potatoes are lightly browned. Sprinkle with 3 green onions, sliced.

make-ahead pizza meatloaves

prep time: 15 minutes | **total time:** 1 hour | **makes** 6 servings

- 1 jar (24 ounces) Prego® Traditional Italian Sauce **or** Prego® Roasted Garlic Parmesan Italian Sauce
- 1½ pounds ground beef
- 1½ cups Pepperidge Farm® Herb Seasoned Stuffing
- 2 eggs, beaten
- 1 medium onion, chopped (about ½ cup)
- ¼ cup chopped green pepper
- 1 teaspoon dried oregano leaves, crushed
- 4 ounces mozzarella cheese, cut into 6 pieces
- ½ cup shredded mozzarella cheese (optional)

1. Heat the oven to 400°F. Mix ¾ cup sauce, beef, stuffing, eggs, onion, pepper and oregano thoroughly and shape firmly into 6 loaves, placing 1 piece cheese in the center of each loaf. Place the loaves into a 13×9×2-inch baking pan.

2. Bake for 25 minutes or until the meatloaves are cooked through. If serving immediately, top with the cheese, if desired, and serve with the remaining sauce (warmed). Or, cool the meatloaves completely. Wrap the meatloaves and refrigerate for up to 3 days. Cover and refrigerate the remaining sauce.

3. Unwrap the meatloaves and place with the remaining sauce in a 12-inch skillet. Cover and heat over medium heat until the meatloaves are hot. Sprinkle with the shredded mozzarella cheese and serve with grated Parmesan cheese, if desired.

tips | Omit or reserve the optional shredded cheese. Assemble the meatloaves and place in a foil baking pan. Top with the remaining sauce. Wrap tightly and freeze for up to 3 months. From frozen, bake, covered, for 1 hour or until the meatloaves are cooked through. Sprinkle with the shredded cheese, if desired.

You can also make 1 large meatloaf instead of 6 smaller meatloaves. Bake for 1 hour or until cooked through.

tater topped casserole

prep time: 10 minutes | **total time:** 35 minutes | **makes** 5 servings

1 pound ground beef

1 medium onion, chopped (about ½ cup)

1 can Campbell's® Condensed Cream of Mushroom Soup **or** Campbell's® Condensed 98% Fat Free Cream of Mushroom Soup

1 tablespoon ketchup

1 tablespoon Worcestershire sauce

3 cups frozen fried potato nuggets

1. Cook the beef and onion in a 10-inch skillet over medium-high heat until the beef is well browned, stirring to separate meat. Pour off any fat.

2. Stir the soup, ketchup and Worcestershire in the skillet. Spoon the beef mixture into a 2-quart shallow baking dish. Arrange the potatoes around the inside edge of the baking dish.

3. Bake at 425°F. for 25 minutes or until the potatoes are golden brown.

tip| Cook the beef mixture as directed and transfer to a baking pan. Let cool completely, wrap tightly and freeze. Top with potatoes before baking. From frozen, bake, uncovered, for 50 minutes or until potatoes are golden brown. Or, thaw in the refrigerator, bake, uncovered, for 35 minutes or until potatoes are golden brown.

tuna noodle casserole

prep time: 20 minutes | **total time:** 45 minutes | **makes** 4 servings

1 can Campbell's® Condensed Cream of Mushroom Soup **or** Campbell's® Condensed 98% Fat Free Cream of Mushroom Soup

½ cup milk

2 tablespoons chopped pimiento (optional)

1 cup frozen green peas

2 cans (about 5 ounces **each**) tuna in water, drained

4 ounces (about 2 cups) medium egg noodles, cooked and drained

2 tablespoons plain dry bread crumbs

1 tablespoon butter, melted

1. Heat the oven to 400°F. Stir the soup, milk, pimientos, if desired, peas, tuna and noodles in a 1½-quart casserole. Stir the bread crumbs and butter in a small bowl.

2. Bake the tuna mixture for 20 minutes or until hot and bubbling. Stir the tuna mixture. Sprinkle with the bread crumb mixture.

3. Bake for 5 minutes or until the bread crumb mixture is golden brown.

tip | For a crunchy, flavorful onion topping, substitute 1 can (2.8 ounces) French's® French Fried Onions (about 1⅓ cups), crushed, for the bread crumb and butter mixture.

hash brown potato casserole

prep time: 10 minutes I **total time:** 1 hour 40 minutes I **makes** 8 servings

1 package (about 30 ounces) frozen country-style hash brown potatoes

1 cup shredded Cheddar cheese (about 4 ounces)

1 container (16 ounces) sour cream

2 cans (10½ ounces **each**) Campbell's® Condensed Cream of Potato Soup

1 small onion, chopped (about ¼ cup)

½ cup grated Parmesan cheese

1. Heat the oven to 350°F. Spray a 3-quart shallow baking dish with vegetable cooking spray.

2. Stir the potatoes, half the Cheddar cheese, the sour cream, soup, onion and Parmesan cheese in a large bowl. Season the potato mixture as desired. Spread the potato mixture in the baking dish. Cover the baking dish.

3. Bake for 45 minutes. Uncover the baking dish. Sprinkle with the remaining Cheddar cheese.

4. Bake, uncovered, for 45 minutes or until the potatoes are tender and the top is lightly browned.

tip | Assemble as directed but do not bake (reserve remaining ½ cup Cheddar cheese for topping). Cover and refrigerate up to 24 hours. To bake, heat the oven to 350°F. Bake, covered, for 45 minutes. Sprinkle with the reserved Cheddar cheese and bake, uncovered, for 45 minutes more.

ultimate chicken pot pie

prep time: 15 minutes | **total time:** 50 minutes | **makes** 6 servings

1 package (about 14 ounces) refrigerated pie crust (2 crusts), at room temperature

1 can Campbell's® Condensed Cream of Chicken Soup **or** Campbell's® Condensed 98% Fat Free Cream of Chicken Soup

½ cup milk

2 cups cubed cooked chicken

1 package (12 ounces) frozen mixed vegetables (carrots, green beans, corn, peas), thawed (about 2⅔ cups)

1 cup shredded Cheddar cheese (about 4 ounces)

1. Heat the oven to 400°F. Line the bottom of a 9-inch pie plate with 1 pie crust. Trim any excess.

2. Stir the soup, milk, chicken and vegetables in a medium bowl. Spoon the chicken mixture into the pie plate. Sprinkle with ¾ cup cheese. Place the remaining pie crust over the filling. Trim any excess. Crimp the edges of the top and bottom crusts together. Using a sharp knife, cut several slits in the top crust.

3. Bake for 35 minutes or until the crust is golden brown. Sprinkle the crust with the remaining cheese.

tip | Omit or reserve ¼ cup cheese as an optional topping. Assemble as directed, wrap tightly and freeze. From frozen, bake, covered, at 400°F. for 1 hour. Uncover. Bake, uncovered, for 45 minutes more or until golden brown. Or, thaw in the refrigerator and bake, covered, for 50 minutes, then uncover and bake for 35 minutes more or until golden brown. Sprinkle with the optional cheese, if desired.

chicken alfredo

prep time: 20 minutes | **total time:** 35 minutes | **makes** 4 servings

2 tablespoons olive oil

1¼ pounds skinless, boneless chicken breast halves, cut into strips

½ teaspoon salt

¼ teaspoon ground black pepper

1 jar (14.5 ounces) Prego® Roasted Garlic Parmesan Alfredo Sauce

8 ounces (½ of a 1-pound package) fettuccine pasta, cooked and drained

2 tablespoons chopped fresh parsley

1. Heat the oil in a 12-inch skillet over medium-high heat. Sprinkle the chicken with the salt and pepper. Add the chicken to the skillet and cook until the chicken is cooked through, stirring occasionally. Remove the chicken from the skillet and keep warm. Reduce the heat to medium.

2. Stir the Alfredo sauce in the skillet and heat through. Add the chicken and fettuccine and toss to coat.

3. Sprinkle with the parsley and serve immediately.

tips| You may substitute 2 packages (about 9 ounces each) refrigerated cooked chicken strips for the fresh chicken and omit Step 1.

For Chicken Bacon Alfredo, stir in ¼ cup crumbled cooked bacon (about 4 slices cooked drained and crumbled) with the sauce.

classic beef stroganoff

prep time: 20 minutes I **total time:** 40 minutes I **makes** 4 servings

1 pound boneless beef sirloin steak **or** beef top round steak, ¾-inch thick (about 1 steak), cut into 2-inch pieces

⅛ teaspoon cracked black pepper

1 tablespoon vegetable oil

1 medium onion, finely chopped (about ½ cup)

1 can Campbell's® Condensed Cream of Mushroom Soup **or** Campbell's® Condensed 98% Fat Free Cream of Mushroom Soup

½ cup water

¼ cup dry sherry (optional)

1 tablespoon tomato paste

¼ cup plain yogurt

8 ounces (about 4 cups) **uncooked** medium egg noodles, cooked and drained

1 tablespoon chopped fresh parsley

1. Season the beef with the black pepper.

2. Heat the oil in a 10-inch skillet over medium-high heat. Add the beef and cook until well browned, stirring often. Remove the beef from the skillet. Pour off any fat.

3. Reduce the heat to medium. Add the onion and cook until tender.

4. Stir in the soup, water, sherry, if desired, and tomato paste and heat to a boil. Return the beef to the skillet and cook until the beef is cooked through. Remove the skillet from the heat. Stir in the yogurt. Serve the beef mixture over the noodles and sprinkle with the parsley.

red wine braised short ribs

prep time: 25 minutes | **total time:** 2 hours 25 minutes | **makes** 6 servings

5 pounds beef short ribs, cut into serving-sized pieces

⅔ cup all-purpose flour

2 tablespoons olive oil

2 large onions, cut in half and sliced (about 2 cups)

2 tablespoons tomato paste

3 large carrots, peeled and cut into 2-inch pieces (about 1½ cups)

2 stalks celery, cut into 2-inch pieces (about 1½ cups)

4 cloves garlic, chopped

1 tablespoon chopped fresh rosemary leaves

4 cups Swanson® Beef Stock

1 cup dry red wine

1. Season the beef with salt and black pepper. Coat the beef with flour.

2. Heat the oil in an 8-quart saucepot over medium-high heat. Add the beef in 2 batches and cook until well browned on all sides. Remove the beef from the saucepot.

3. Add the onions and tomato paste to the saucepot and cook for 5 minutes, stirring occasionally. Stir in the carrots, celery, chopped garlic and rosemary and cook for 3 minutes. Stir in the stock, wine and remaining flour and heat to a boil. Return the beef to the saucepot. Reduce the heat to low. Cover and cook for 1 hour 30 minutes or until the beef is fork-tender.

tomato beef stew with red wine

prep time: 10 minutes | **total time:** 1 hour 10 minutes | **makes** 4 servings

- 1 pound boneless beef chuck roast **or** sirloin, cut into ¾-inch pieces
- 2 tablespoons vegetable oil
- 1 large onion, chopped (about 1 cup)
- 2 cloves garlic, minced
- 1 cup dry red wine (we like pinot noir)
- 1 jar (24 ounces) Prego® Fresh Mushroom Italian Sauce
- 1 bag (16 ounces) frozen peas and carrots

1. Season the beef as desired. Heat 1 tablespoon oil in a 12-inch skillet over medium-high heat. Add the beef and cook until well browned, stirring occasionally (the browning is key to the flavor in this recipe). Remove the beef from the skillet.

2. Heat the remaining oil in the skillet. Add the onion and garlic and cook and stir for 5 minutes or until lightly browned. Increase the heat to high. Add the wine and cook for 2 minutes or until the wine is reduced by half, stirring to scrape up the browned bits from the bottom of the skillet.

3. Stir in the sauce and heat to a boil. Return the beef to the skillet. Reduce the heat to low. Cover and cook for 35 minutes or until the beef is fork-tender. Stir in the vegetables and cook, uncovered, for 2 minutes or until hot. Season to taste.

chicken with savory lemon caper sauce

prep time: 10 minutes | **total time:** 30 minutes | **makes** 4 servings

1¼ pounds skinless, boneless chicken breast halves

2 tablespoons canola oil

1 large shallot, chopped (about ¼ cup)

2 tablespoons rinsed drained capers

1 tablespoon all-purpose flour

1½ cups Swanson® Chicken Broth **or** Swanson® Certified Organic Chicken Broth **or** Swanson® Natural Goodness® Chicken Broth

1 tablespoon lemon juice

2 tablespoons stone ground mustard

3 tablespoons half and half

1. Season the chicken as desired.

2. Heat half the oil in a 12-inch skillet over medium-high heat. Add the chicken and cook for 6 minutes or until browned on both sides. Remove the chicken from the skillet.

3. Reduce the heat to medium. Heat the remaining oil in the skillet. Add the shallot and capers and cook for 2 minutes, stirring occasionally. Add the flour and cook and stir for 1 minute.

4. Stir the broth, lemon juice and mustard in a bowl. Stir the broth mixture in the skillet and cook until the mixture boils and thickens. Reduce the heat to low. Return the chicken to the skillet. Cook for 5 minutes or until the chicken is cooked through. Remove the skillet from the heat. Stir in the half and half. Season to taste.

tip | Serve the chicken and sauce over hot cooked noodles or rice.

honey garlic chicken

prep time: 10 minutes | **total time:** 30 minutes | **makes** 4 servings

1¼ pounds skinless, boneless chicken breast halves, cut into 1-inch pieces

2 tablespoons olive oil

1 teaspoon minced garlic

3 cups broccoli florets

1 tablespoon reduced sodium soy sauce

2 tablespoons honey

¼ teaspoon crushed red pepper

½ cup water

1 can Campbell's® Condensed Cream of Mushroom Soup or Campbell's® Condensed 98% Fat Free Cream of Mushroom Soup

3 cups hot cooked brown rice or white rice

1 green onion, sliced (about 2 tablespoons)

2 tablespoons sliced almonds, toasted

1. Season the chicken as desired.

2. Heat the oil in a 12-inch skillet over medium-high heat. Add the chicken and cook until browned, stirring occasionally. Add the garlic and cook and stir for 1 minute. Add the broccoli and cook until tender-crisp, stirring occasionally.

3. Stir the soy sauce, honey, red pepper, water and soup in the skillet and heat to a boil. Reduce the heat to low. Cover and cook for 3 minutes or until the chicken is cooked through. Season to taste. Serve the chicken mixture over the rice. Sprinkle with the green onion and almonds.

tip | For a spicier dish, add more crushed red pepper.

super moist pork chops

prep time: 5 minutes | **total time:** 25 minutes | **makes** 4 servings

- 1 tablespoon vegetable oil
- 4 bone-in pork chops, ½-inch thick (about 1½ pounds)
- 1 can (10¾ ounces) Campbell's® Condensed Golden Mushroom Soup
- ¼ cup water

1. Heat the oil in a 10-inch skillet over medium-high heat. Add the pork and cook until well browned on both sides.

2. Stir the soup and water in the skillet and heat to a boil. Reduce the heat to low. Cover and cook for 10 minutes or until the pork is cooked through.